girl who thinks too much.

IN THE ECHOES OF MY SILENCE
I FOUND MY VOICE.

RITIKA KARAMCHANDANI

FOR EVERY GIRL WHO THINKS TOO MUCH, THERE'S POETRY THAT SPEAKS FOR HER.

In a world that often tells her to stop overthinking, she finds strength in her ability to analyze, to question, to feel deeply. She is the girl who thinks too much, who sees the world through a lens of endless possibilities and potential pitfalls.

Her poetry reflects the duality of her existence—both a blessing and a curse, a source of inspiration and a well of uncertainty.

But in every line, there is a glimpse of the beauty she sees in the world, even when it's clouded by doubt.

WORDS UNSPOKEN

Let me tell you this,my life hasn't been easy these days.
These Days, Days aren't really days.
They are just annoying obstacles that need to be faced.

Everything takes so much energy.
People around me don't understand,
I'm doing the best I can.

I feel I'm turning numb,
things I previously enjoyed no longer hold me the same fun.

All I Have one person by my side
And I'm not sure these problems will ever abide.

Behind my smile is a weeping heart,
behind my laugh I'm falling apart.

Look closely at me and you will see,
the girl I am, it isn't really me.

Behind my smile is a weeping heart,
behind my laugh I'm falling apart.
Look closely at me and you will see,
the girl I am, it isn't really me.

SILENT SCREAMS

I have been here before,
the world never observes but ignores.

The beauty inside me had died
So I wore a mask that always smiled.

To hide my feelings behind a lie,
Each and every day I had to suffer a sigh .

It feels as though the world becomes
a worse place to be with every passing day,
Nobody wants to hear the pain and
I find isolation as my best way!

It's been this way for months.
Things aren't as they seem.

All I've learned in these times is that
Silence is the most powerful scream!

It's been this way for months.
Things aren't as they seem.
All I've learned in these times is that
Silence is the most powerful scream!

BEHIND A MASK

The me you see isn't the real me
This is not what I wish to be.

I no longer chase anyone or anything
I feel abandoned in my despair,
and it's difficult for me to repair.

I get broken each day some more,
I want the old me that i adore

Behind all my smiles there are tears,
Behind all the comforts there are fears

People will never know how i feel,
They never even ask
So I have decided
To live behind a mask.

People will never know how i feel,
They never even ask
So I have decided
To live behind a mask.

HEARTACHE

why is life such a heartache what did I do to deserve it
sometimes it makes me wonder if living is even worth it

'cause every time I get somewhere
I go right back to the beginning
seems no matter how hard I try
there's never no place for winning

but I pick up the broken pieces every time they shatter
and then I go on with my life like nothing a matter

why is life such a heartache
what did I do to deserve it
sometimes it makes me wonder
if living is even worth it

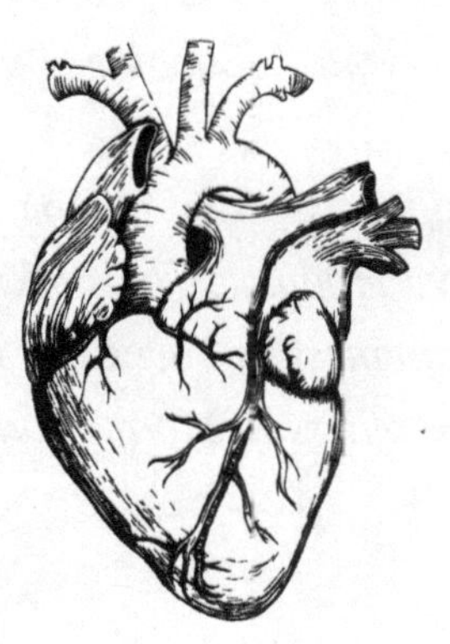

DARK PLACE

The World Seems To Be A Dark Place.
Place Where Faith Is A Delusion
And Loyalty Is An Illusion!

A Place Where Everyone Is Self Centered
And Everything Is A Joke.
Places Where Feelings Don't Matter, We've Entered.

Everything Has Become A Lie
And I Know Nobody's Gonna Deny!
There's Peace Left At Nothing,
Everyone Is Sobbing And Craving For Happiness.

Happiness, Real Happiness Is Dancing In The Rain,
Real Happiness Is Walking With No Pain
Happiness In Faces I've Longed To See,
Happiness Is More Than Being Free.

Real Happiness Is Dancing In The Rain,
Real Happiness Is Walking With No Pain
Happiness In Faces I've Longed To See,
Happiness Is More Than Being Free.

SELF PORTRAY

I use to have many friends, way back some day
But with the moving time, They All slipped away.
Its not like it's their fault, I've Done it on my own
Isolated Myself from everyone, All I wanted was to be alone.

While everybody was busy selecting their priority lists
I was confused by all the trust issues that exists.
All I do now is to crave for a true mate
Who'll accept me without hesitate.

Of course, there are acquaintances I see most every day
Share moments of trivial bullshit, flash smiles along the way
Maybe some of them really listen to what I actually say
But, most of them only find time for the girl my mind makes me portray

All I do now is to crave for a true mate
Who'll accept me without hesitate.

BEHIND A SMILE

I'm the girl who hides behind a smile.
Who's lost among her thoughts in a pile.

It's amazing how things do change,
When people let you down.
And how that once happy face can
Turns into an arrogant frown.

People you live with, change you a lot
Some try to control you and make you who you're not.

Let me go where I wish. I don't want any regrets in my life.
Even if I strive, I'll fail, I'll learn ,I'll grow,
I will survive.

People you live with, change you a lot
Some try to control you and make
you who you're not.

LONG YEAR

It’s been a long year
It's been a long year
Full of ups and downs and tears
But the best is that you've overcome all your fears.

Always tried to give your best,
Lots of lessons and plans and projects,
Now it's time for you to rest.

It feels like it all started yesterday,
Went school, made friends ,had a bae
And look now where we are today!

Lost all friends, Lost all will,
Lost all hope and peace and thrill,
Here we are all alone, looking at the moon and standing still!

Alcohol replaced family, cigarettes replaced friends,
From sharing secrets to crying alone,
Each thing taught that everything ends!

It feels like it all started yesterday,
Went school, made friends ,had a bae
And look now where we are today!

DO YOU KNOW?

Where do I go When I'm feeling so lost
and I don't want to be found?
For every time that I broke down
There is a fake smile to cover the frown.

Where do I go when the times get rough?
I hide behind lies when things get tough
Force myself to think it was enough.

Where do I go when I'm trying to laugh but all I can do is cry?
Thinking of old good times and getting sad by looking at the sky.

Where do i go when I pick up the broken pieces every time they shatter ?
Then I go on with my life like that, nothing matter..

Where do I go, where do I go?
Do you know?

Where do I go when I'm trying to
laugh but all I can do is cry?
Thinking of old good times and
getting sad by looking at the sky.

WHAT'S HOME?

People can never be home,
They always change, become unknown.

The more you care, the more you suffer
Every time you try , it keeps getting tougher.

Stop trying, Stop crying
Can't you see, you're internally dying.

All this pain, has no gain
You need to love yourself once again.

All this pain, has no gain
You need to love yourself once again.

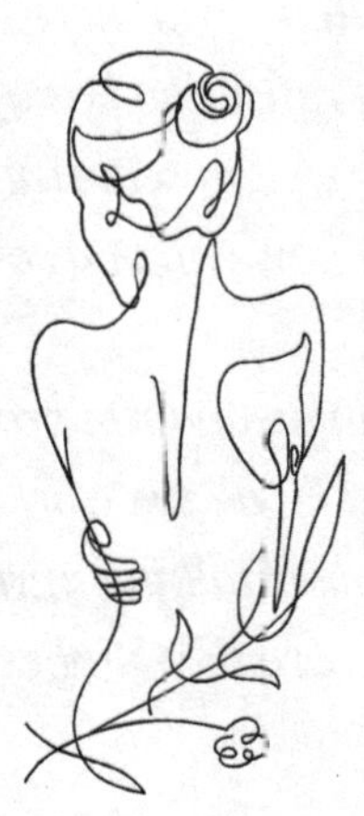

MIRROR AND ME

My mirror spoke to me,
Said the cake from last week,
Is starting to show on the hips.
Chubby cheeks and teeth within,
How must I hide my double chin?

Closet overflowing with long sleeve tees,
Flabby arms should be hidden, I plead.

Hold up, wait here, why would I care,
My reflection has opinions all unfair.
My weight scale might dip boo,
But how will you save your drowning IQ?

Chin up and run proud girl,
And let all the world disappear in a blur.
So dear talking mirror on the wall,
You are the dumbest of them all.

My weight scale might dip boo,
But how will you save your drowning IQ?

DREAMS

Sometimes I feel is it reality or just my dreams?
Nobody feels safe and I internally scream.

Everything i see these days give me pain,
It seems all my efforts are always in vain.

There's a cliff named OVERTHINKING
& I'm standing on the edge
I try to overcome , i try , i try and i will, i pledge.

Everything i see these days give me pain,
It seems all my efforts are always in vain.

IS THIS ME?

Never knew this was what I had to see,
I was taken away even from me.

But as the time passes by I understand
Everything happens as it is planned.

Today,i feel I'm more than one can imagine
I love myself as I see myself growing.
I've no friendships and no enmities
I think I'm at my best, maybe?

When I'm lonely I find an opportunity
To meet myself with unscathed clarity.
I can then verify if I have been true,
To myself , or am i rue?

I now stop and greet my reflection,
All i ever wanted was my own love.
I've always been rough to myself
But now It is the time to put myself above.

So revel in your loneliness while you can,
It's not forever, only for a short span.

Never knew this was what I had to see,
I was taken away even from me.

TOO MUCH ON MY MIND

There's too much on my mind,
But there's not enough time,
To write it all down,
So I guess I'll just drown.

Each moment's a blur,
A chaotic detour,
But amidst all the strive,
I'm just living my life.

Faking a smile, with a fake shine
I'm holding up my tears, facing all my fears
This time I'm getting weak
and I fear all my thoughts are going to leak.

Once they come out , I'll be unable to face the crowd.
Till then The mask i wear , is the new me
Life will go as it is planned to be!

Faking a smile, with a fake shine
I'm holding up my tears, facing all my fears

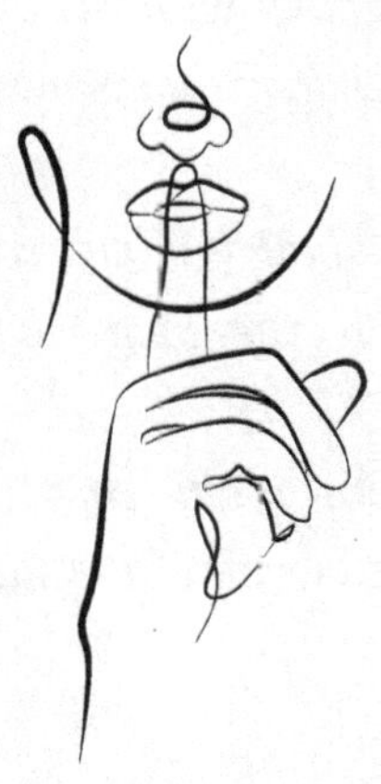

LOVE ME

I know it ain't easy to love me,
But I'm trying my best what i could be.

With every step forward, and each word I say,
I'm learning and growing, finding my way.

I wear my heart on a tattered sleeve,
Hoping you'll see the best in me.

Together we'll write our story's page,
With love that grows, age to age.

For though it ain't easy, love's a dance,
With every step, we find our chance.

I know it ain't easy, but please, take my hand,
We'll weather the storms, together we'll stand.

I know it ain't easy, but please, take my hand,
We'll weather the storms, together we'll stand.

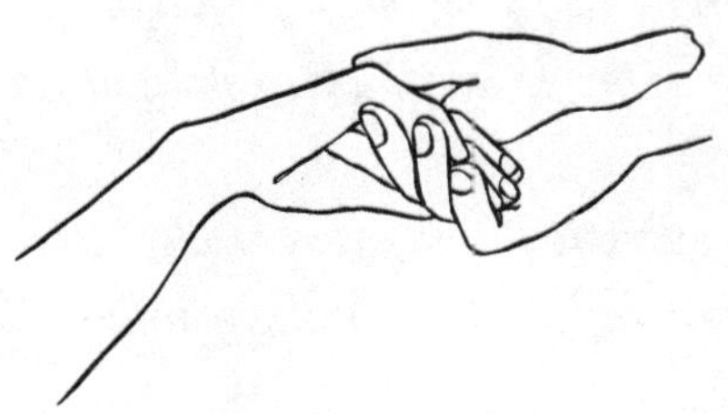

WHO AM I?

That's something I wonder every day,
From being delighted to feeling dismayed.
Emotions twist in a constant spree,
Such highs and lows are normal for me.

In the morning light, I find my cheer,
But shadows creep, bringing back my fear.
I question the balance, the highs and lows,
As the river of life continuously flows.

One moment, joy, like a bird on the wing,
The next, a sorrow, a deep, silent sting.
Emotions swing like a pendulum's sway,
From bright sunshine to skies of grey.

In every tear and every smile,
I find my strength, mile by mile.

In the morning light, I find my cheer,
But shadows creep, bringing back my fear.
I question the balance, the highs and lows,
As the river of life continuously flows.

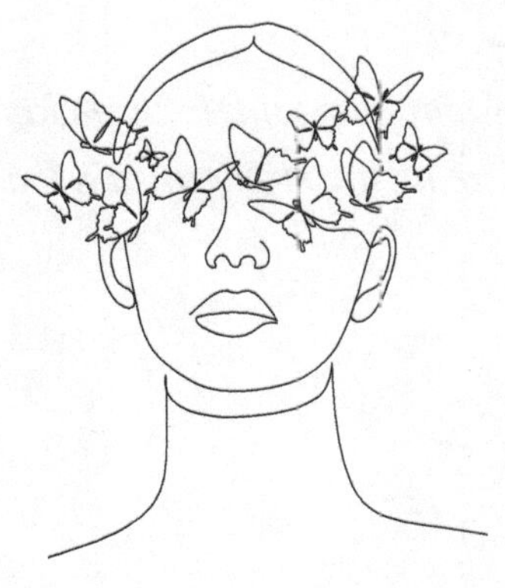

ME

I question every single move,
And every step I take to prove,

So I must learn to quiet my mind,
And leave the overthinking behind,

To trust that I'll make the right choice,
And to let go of that inner voice.

For in the silence, truths unfold,
And courage blooms, brave and bold.

Embracing faith in the unknown,
I found my strength, and I've grown.

I must learn to quiet my mind,
And leave the overthinking behind,

To trust that I'll make the right choice,
And to let go of that inner voice.

THOUGHTS

Like a pendulum, my thoughts swing,
Back and forth, like an endless ring,
In my mind, they always sling,
In this motion, no peace they bring.

In the quiet, I'll break free,
From the cycle that eats me.
To steady my mind and let it soar
Finding solace on a peaceful shore.

I wish for calm, a moment's rest,
To clear my head and feel less stressed,
To find a place where I can breathe,
And let these restless thoughts take leave

In the quiet, I'll break free,
From the cycle that eats me.
To steady my mind and let it soar
Finding solace on a peaceful shore.

THE PATH

Every path I take, leads me back to the start,
In the maze of overthinking, I'm losing heart.

Yet, amidst the chaos, a spark of light,
A glimmer of hope, breaking through the night.

For even in the darkest hour,
Hope will bloom like a timeless flower.

I'll trust that in this endless fight,
The spark will lead me to the light.

So I'll hold on to that shining ray,
And trust that it'll lead me where I need to stay.

In the midst of doubts and endless fray,
I'll find my path and be okay.

Every path I take, leads me back to the start,
In the maze of overthinking, I'm losing heart.

INTERNAL STORM

In the depths of my heart, a storm does rage,
Emotions and thoughts, clashing in a cage.

With every breath, I'll calm the storm,
And find a place where I can be warm.

Thunder rolls with a mighty sound,
Echoes of fears that shake the ground.

Yet through the tempest, a whisper grows,
A promise of peace that gently flows.

As the storm subsides and clarity appears,
I embrace the calm, release my fears.

As the storm subsides and clarity appears,
I embrace the calm, release my fears.

DO YOU LOVE ME ANYMORE?

I feel like I'm caged these days,
Lost my freedom, in a haze.
For even a little love, I need to thrive,
But your heart feels like a distant dive.

I don't think you love me anymore,
What's keeping us together? What for?

I don't recognize you these days,
This isn't the man I always loved.
The spark in your eyes has faded away,
The warmth in your touch feels so far away.

The laughter we shared has turned to sighs,
The dreams we built are seeming like lies.

For love should set us free, not chain us down,
But here I am, feeling lost, about to drown.
I search for your heart but find it cold,
Our story's ending, left untold.

I search for your heart but find it cold,
Our story's ending, left untold.

SILENT SCREAMS

Can't you hear my silent screams?
They are so loud they echo in my dreams.

Behind this mask of a cheerful disguise
Stretches a gloomy path, endless in lies.

For years my voiceless cries have been,
But they always fall on ears that don't listen.

What can I share? These cries lack voice,
Only waves of sadness and darkness without choice.

I can't convey how this feels; it's beyond extreme,
So I keep my lips sealed to stifle my unspoken screams.

Can't you hear my silent screams?
They are so loud they echo in my dreams.

MY UNKNOWN SCARS

Here on my thigh is a mark I engraved.
In my darkest moment, a blade I braved,

Punishing my body for feeling so flawed,
Here lies my confession ,for i don't feel applaud.

I feel guilty for leaving this sign,
A constant reminder of when I was not fine.

But seeing these scars helps me see
That I survived so much trauma and now I am free.

So I ask you now to join me in this fight,
To show those demons they have no right.

Here on my thigh lies a mark of survival,
I conquered my darkness, defeated my rival.

Here on my thigh is a mark I engraved.
In my darkest moment, a blade I braved,
Punishing my body for feeling so flawed,
Here lies my confession ,for i don't feel applaud.

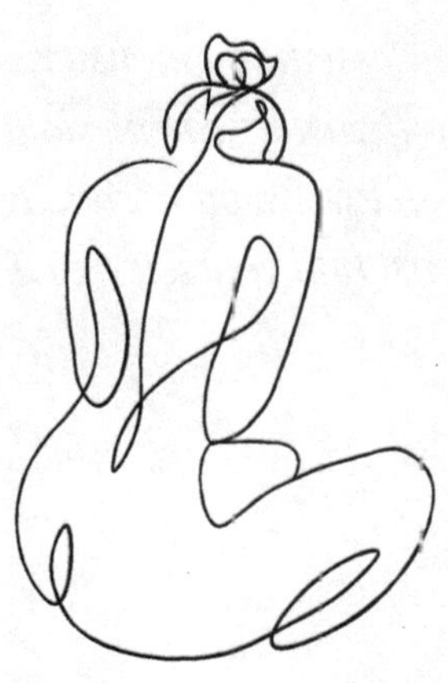

DEPRESSION

Depression is a monster
That destroys both heart and soul.
It tortures without mercy
And consumes the victim whole.

It whispers lies so cruel,
In the shadows it will hide,
Stealing all your joy,
Till there's nothing left inside.

Depression is a monster,
But monsters can be slain.
With love, support, and patience,
You'll find yourself again.

Depression is a monster,
But monsters can be slain.
With love, support, and patience,
You'll find yourself again.

SOMETIMES

Sometimes I can't find the words
That fills my messy head.
Can't find the effort to smile
Or get out of my silly old bed.

The world can seem so foreign,
A place where I don't belong,
And even when I try my best,
A smile doesn't stay for long.

I could wear a happy mask,
Pretend I'm full of cheer,
Yet in a crowd of faces,
I feel the loneliness near.

Unsure of the answers,
Uncertain if I care,
To face another day here,
In this recurring nightmare.

Unsure of the answers,
Uncertain if I care,
To face another day here,
In this recurring nightmare.

WHAT DO YOU SEE IN ME?

When you look at me, What do you see?
If you look closely, You'll see through me.

Gaze deep into my eyes, And you'll forget my lies.
You'll see my pain, If you look again.

Do you know how it feels to cry alone at night?
What you see on the outside Is not who I am inside.

I'm broken within, Even if it's hidden.
So look at me again. What do you see?

I'm broken within, Even if it's hidden.
So look at me again. What do you see?

LIFE JOURNEY

To learn as a child
What life is meant to be,
To know it's more than just myself,
It's much bigger than me.

To overcome the tragedies,
To survive the hardest times.
To face those moments filled with pain,
And still manage to be kind.

To be proud of my choices,
To give my all each day,
To take what God has given me,
And make it more in every way.

take what God has given you,
And make it more in every way.

PERFECTION

Perfection was made to make us feel flawed,
but being imperfect is truly perfect, after all.

We spend every hour and day,
every week and month, trying to stand out,
to be different from the bunch.

We naturally seek answers to life's big questions,
like what perfection means, and why it causes such tension.

You chase after "perfection," a concept that's unclear, but it's
better to be yourself and let go of that fear.

Happiness should matter more than a word like "perfection,"
so think about this: who really shows in your reflection?

Perfection was made to make us feel flawed,
but being imperfect is truly perfect, after all.

IS IT ONLY ME?

Staring at the ceiling, I can't believe how I'm feeling,
Wanting to cry, it's hard, I'm grieving,
Pillow over my face, trying to hide my breathing.

It's 2am, and I'm wide awake,
Thinking about all my mistakes,
Wondering why we had to break,
And if I can handle this ache.

You were the one I adored,
The one who made me sure,
My forever, my one,
But now you've left me undone.

You were the one I adored,
The one who made me sure,
My forever, my one,
But now you've left me undone.

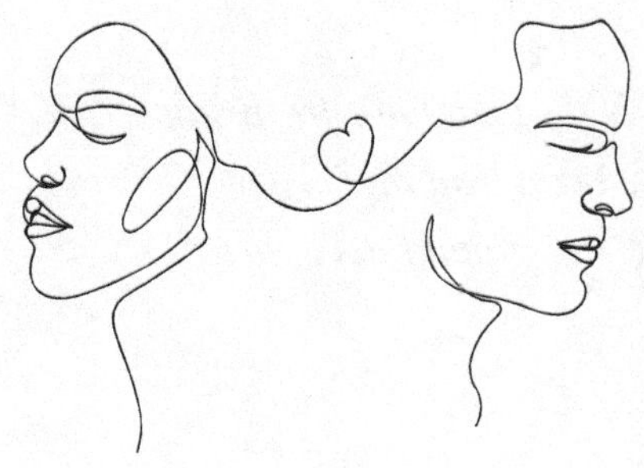

NEW ME

I lie awake tonight,
Reflecting on what could be changed.
I try to reassure myself, But it all feels so strange.

Is it me, Or is it you?
Should I keep trying, Or are we through?

We've shared so much time,
Yet now we part ways.
The pain of leaving
Makes me want to stay.

Is this the end, Or a fresh start?
Only I can lead me
When my mind falls apart.

Is it me, Or is it you?
Should I keep trying, Or are we through?

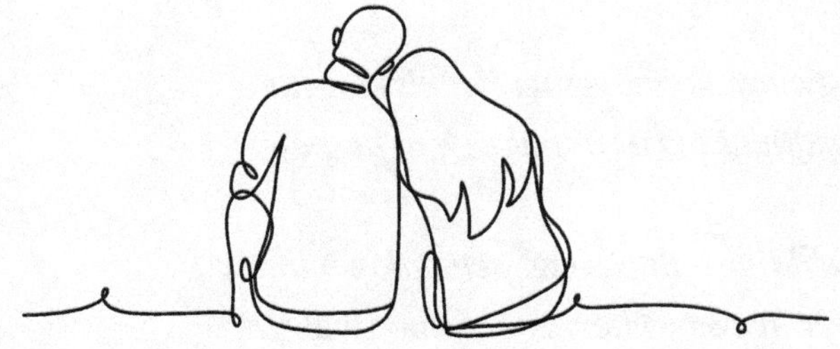

THE SONG YOU WROTE

He crafted a song, but it was left incomplete
Their love bloomed fast, then faced defeat

She's on his bed, tears streaming in his lap
He's crying too, knowing there's no turning back.

Time ticks by, and neither can accept
That letting go might be their best bet

As the day ends, he faces his greatest fear
To part from her, not a single tear.

No more goodbyes with a kiss to share
Just thinking of it makes him despair

He'll finish that song, pen it down today
And In every line, her memory will stay.

Time ticks by, and neither can accept
That letting go might be our best bet

WHAT I WANT

I want to run, I want to flee,
From the shadows of what I used to be.
I want to heal, I want to mend,
But this heartache will not end.

I want to break free from the chains
Of the love that left me with only pains.
I want to rebuild, I want to soar,
But I'm haunted by memories of before.

He left a scar, the wound runs deep
Promises broken, secrets he'd keep.
All the trust he tossed away
Echoes in my mind, day by day.

How can I mend this broken heart?
Find a way to make a fresh start?
He's gone, but his ghost remains
And I'm left with these endless chains.

I want to run, I want to flee,
From the shadows of what I used to be.

SOUL ON FIRE

How do I mend this shattered soul?
My world is fractured, out of control.
My heart aches with echoes of our time,
of moments shared, so pure, are like sunshine.

My nights are haunted by your sweet embrace,
I wake alone, with tears on my face.
Each day is a struggle to find my way,
as I am filled with memories that won't fade away.

How do I heal and make a brand new start,
when the love of my life has left my heart?

How do I heal and make a brand new start,
when the love of my life has left my heart?

JOURNEY

In the journey we all share,
With ups and downs, here and there,
Life's a path both rough and sweet,
With every friend and foe we meet.

Through sunny days and stormy nights,
We chase our dreams, we fight our fights,
Love and laughter, joy and pain,
We rise, we fall, and rise again.

So hold on tight, don't lose your way,
Keep hope alive, come what may,
For in our hearts, the light will glow,
Together strong, we'll always grow.

Hold on tight, don’t lose your way,
Keep hope alive, come what may,
For in our hearts, the light will glow,
Together strong, we'll always grow.

IF I COULD

I know I'm lost, and so are you,
I know our days are painted blue.
I know I've made mistakes, it's true,
I know the pain I've caused to you.

I know I'm shattered, piece by piece,
I know my pride won't bring me peace.

I know I'm fleeting, just a spark,
I know I'm wandering in the dark.
I know I'm broken beyond repair,
But could you mend me with your care?

If you could hold my trembling hand,
Whisper words that understand.

If you could heal this aching heart,
If you could mend it, piece by part.
If I was different, whole inside,
If I was free from fear and pride.

If I was joyful, full of grace, If I was...you'd love my face?

I know I'm broken beyond repair,
But could you mend me with your care?

WHY CAN'T I?

Day by day, Miles apart,
I hold you close Within my heart.

My heart says stay, My mind says go,
Torn between What I know.
Remembering when We were friends,
How it started And how it ends.

I begged for a chance, A way to make things right,
But you turned away, Vanished into the night.
Now tears fall freely, Staining my soul,
Wondering why you left me, Why I can't feel whole.

Why can't I move on,
Find someone new? When all I do is think Of you.

My tears fall freely, Staining the soul,
Wondering why you left me,
Why I can't feel whole.

YOU AND ME

I'm lost in love, but feel so strained,
Holding on through all this pain.

I've tried so hard to make you see,
How much you mean to me.

I love you deeply, that's my plight,
But it seems you don't feel right.

It's painful to love you this way,
Knowing you might not stay.

Why am I chasing shadows, dear?
Why do I keep you so near?

I can't explain this endless ache,
But I'll hold on for your sake.

It's painful to love you this way,
Knowing you might not stay.

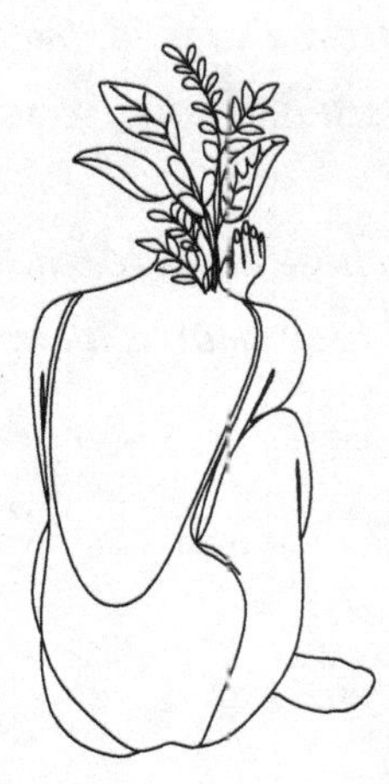

WHY HER?

Promises made, now turned to dust,
What I believed, was lost in mistrust.

You locked my heart, gave her the key,
Now you're with her, not with me.

It seemed so real, this love we knew,
Yet here I am, alone and blue.

The tears I've shed, the pain I've faced,
All trust and hope, so sadly erased.

You chose her love, with me as the cost,
Now I see clearly, all hope is lost.

You chose her love, with me as the cost,
Now I see clearly, all hope is lost.

WHEN YOU LEFT

My world feels empty, colors fade to grey,
Breathing is heavy, lost in dismay.

The light has vanished, shadows remain,
Consuming me in an endless pain.

Heart shattered on the floor,
Tears still fall, I watch the door.

I need you here, can't you see?
Without you, I'm not me.

I need you here, can't you see?
Without you, I'm not me.

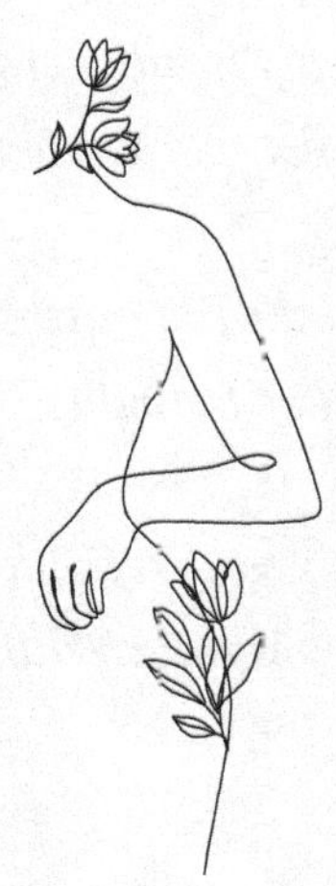

THE GIRL WHO THINKS TOO MUCH

She walks alone in quiet thought,
In every dream, a battle fought.

Her mind's a maze, a winding path,
A sea of questions, aftermath.

She wonders why the sky's so blue,
And why the stars are never true.

Her heart is full, her mind's a storm,
Yet in her words, there's something warm.

She thinks too much, they often say,
But in her thoughts, she finds her way.

A poet's soul, a thinker's mind,
In every verse, a truth she'll find.

For she's the girl who thinks too much,
But in her words, there's magic's touch.
Her thoughts are wild, her heart is free,
In overthinking, she finds her key.